Scientists who have changed the world

Isaac
Newton

by Michael White

OTHER TITLES IN THE SERIES
Alexander Graham Bell by Michael Pollard (1-85015-200-4)
Charles Darwin by Anna Sproule (1-85015-213-6)
Thomas Edison by Anna Sproule (1-85015-201-2)
Albert Einstein by Fiona Macdonald (1-85015-253-5)
Alexander Fleming by Beverley Birch (1-85015-184-9)
Galileo Galilei by Michael White (1-85015-277-6)
Johann Gutenberg by Michael Pollard (1-85015-255-1)
Guglielmo Marconi by Beverley Birch (1-85015-185-7)
Margaret Mead by Michael Pollard (1-85015-228-4)
James Watt by Anna Sproule (1-85015-254-3)
The Wright Brothers by Anna Sproule (1-85015-229-2)

Picture Credits:
Ann Ronan Picture Library: 38; Bridgeman Art Library: 15, 16, 28, 59; by permission of The British Library: 31 (left); by permission of the Syndics of Cambridge University Library: 43; E T Archive: 11; Exley Publications: 33; Lincolnshire County Council: 12, 14, 34; The Mansell Collection: 20, 54; Mary Evans Picture Library: 7, 13, 25; Michael Holford Photographs: 37 (below), 52-53, 53 (below); Millbrook House Ltd. (P.B. Whitehouse): 48 (above); The Museum of London: 26-27; NASA: 30, 31 (right); National Trust Photographic Library/Tessa Musgrave: 45; Paul Brierley: 22, 44; PSA Photo Services: 56-57; Robin Wilson: 60; Royal Society (photograph by Professor Roy Bishop, Acadia University, Nova Scotia, Canada): 13 (above); Scala: 41; Science Photo Library: 4 (NASA), 5 (Mikki Rain), 9 (Alexander Tsiaras), 18 (David Parker), 36 (NOAO), 37 (Dr. John Lorre); ZEFA: 8, 48 (below), 49. Cover: Jeremy Whitaker, by permission of Lord Portsmouth and The Trustees of the Portsmouth Estates.

Published in Great Britain in 1991
by Exley Publications Ltd,
16 Chalk Hill, Watford,
Herts WD1 4BN, United Kingdom.

Copyright © Exley Publications, 1991
Copyright © Michael White, 1990
Reprinted 1993.

A copy of the CIP data is available from
the British Library on request.

ISBN 1-85015-243-8

Series editor: Helen Exley
Picture research: Veneta Bullen
Editing: Samantha Armstrong and
    Margaret Montgomery
Typeset by Brush Off Studios, St Albans.
Printed and bound in Hungary.

Isaac Newton

The story of one of the greatest mathematicians who changed our perception of the universe

Michael White

 EXLEY

The problem of gravity

It was a warm late summer afternoon in 1666. A young man with a book under his arm strolled into the orchard of his mother's house in Woolsthorpe, Lincolnshire in England and sat down beneath a tree to concentrate on his studies. As he flicked the pages of his book, something was stirring above his head in the branches of the tree. The most famous apple in history was just about to fall and set in motion a chain of events that would change the world of science, for ever.

A moment later the apple fell and landed on the head of the twenty-three-year-old Isaac Newton. No doubt it hurt for a moment, but it also set the young scientist thinking.

It just so happened that on that very day, Isaac was struggling with the problem of what it was that kept the moon in its orbit around the earth and the planets in their courses around the sun. It was only after he had thought about why the apple had fallen to the earth, hitting his head on the way, that he really began to have the answer to these problems – the theory of gravity.

"The Miraculous Year"

1666 had been an astonishing year. Only weeks earlier the Great Fire of London had swept away the last remnants of the plague that had taken thousands of lives in the cities. Isaac Newton was a student at Cambridge University, but he had to stay with his mother in the country for over a year as Cambridge, too, was ravaged by the plague. In the country, Newton could enjoy solitude and

Opposite: A view of the Earth taken by astronauts orbiting the Moon. The calculations needed to successfully complete the 500,000 mile round trip are based on the law of gravitation discovered by Isaac Newton.
Below: An artist's impression of the moment an apple fell on Newton's head. When he was an old man he claimed that it was this incident that gave him the inspiration for his great discovery.

relative safety. In the peace and tranquillity, he could concentrate on the scientific problems that he had been grappling with throughout his post graduate years. Already his work was bearing fruit.

During the past year, Isaac Newton had made incredible breakthroughs in mathematics and physics. In 1665, he had found the answer to a problem which had eluded mathematicians for years – what later became known as the binomial theorem.

Later he began work on what was to turn into the greatest development in the history of mathematics – calculus. Today, scientists use both of these theorems in computer programs. Space engineers use calculus and the binomial theorem to help solve complex mathematical problems, such as those involved in making sure that rockets arrive on the moon over 240,000 miles away and return safely to earth. Economists use these branches of mathematics to predict what happens to currencies around the world and the economic state of different nations.

Newton was a mathematical genius who, by his early twenties, had been through the work of every notable mathematician in the world. Then, when he had exhausted current knowledge, he began developing his own theorems and methods to create a mathematical foundation for his scientific work.

Now, here he was, less than twelve months later and on the verge of his greatest discovery of all. When Isaac Newton became world famous, writers looked back on this short period in the Lincolnshire countryside and called it "The Miraculous Year".

Newton's world

In the seventeenth century, science was in its infancy. In the world into which Isaac Newton was born there were many well-educated people who still believed in witchcraft and sorcery. Almost nothing was known about the fundamental principles behind the way many things worked. To most people, the universe was controlled by an all-powerful deity and many observed events and

phenomena were caused by spirits and inexplicable mystical forces. There were no proper theories of mechanics or ideas about how and why things moved the way they did. Scientists knew very little about light and how it behaves, and subjects like chemistry and medicine were based more on magic than science. So, it should come as little surprise that nobody really understood how the planets and the moon kept in their orbits or why it was that falling apples always moved down to the earth. Yet, by the end of Isaac Newton's life he would have the answers to all these things and completely change the way people saw the world.

So famous did this Lincolnshire lad become that, during the scientist's own lifetime, the British poet Alexander Pope coined the popular phrase "Nature, and Nature's Laws lay hid in night. God said: 'Let Newton be!' And all was Light."

Isaac Newton may not have realized it at the time, but the work he began in "The Miraculous Year" would form the basis of the whole of

Isaac Newton was born into a society that still believed in witchcraft. Most of the population were illiterate, very few people knew anything of science and explained even the simplest phenomena by resorting to spirits and demons. In this picture, an old woman is being arrested as a suspected witch. It has been estimated that during the sixteenth and seventeenth centuries over one million people were tortured and executed for being witches.

When expert billiard players compete in a tournament they use their experience and years of practice at estimating forces and angles to get the balls into the pockets. However, using Newton's laws of motion to estimate each shot, it would be possible for a computer to be programmed to be a world champion billiard player.

mathematics and physics for the next three hundred years. Within three centuries of that apple landing on his head, men would land on the moon and send machines to distant planets using his theorems and discoveries. For, modern science is founded on the work of this great man, so much so in fact that whole areas of physics and mathematics are called "Newtonian" after him.

The versatile scientist

Perhaps Isaac Newton's greatest discovery were the laws of motion which explain how forces act upon objects, whether moving or stationary. And, by applying these laws to any mechanical system, it is possible to predict the effect a force will have on any object. If, for example, the weight and speed of two billiard balls are known, by applying Newton's laws, the effect one ball will have on the other, if the snooker player applies a particular

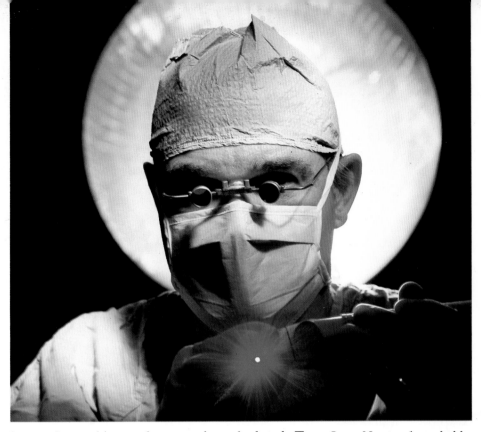

force when taking a shot, can be calculated. Together these laws are used in all areas of science – from designing cars and boats to predicting the course of spaceships going to the moon, from building aircraft engines to making aerodynamic skateboards. Newton also worked out a theory of gravity to explain how the planets travel around the sun. The same theory explained why it is that we do not all float off into space, but instead remain held firmly to the earth.

Newton also worked in many other areas of physics. His theories of light have helped scientists and engineers to design better telescopes and microscopes, spectacles and cameras. His discoveries in optics have led to inventions such as television and lasers. Armed with these theories, future generations of physicists could develop Newton's ideas into the machines and devices we all use today.

The story of how he came to make these monumental discoveries began a few feet away from

Isaac Newton is probably best known for his theory of gravity, but he also made great discoveries in the study of light. Newton's work has played a very important role in creating twentieth century technology. Here a surgeon uses a laser during an eye operation. Lasers are becoming increasingly important tools in medicine and if it were not for Newton's work in optics they might never have been invented.

the famous apple tree in his mother's garden in Lincolnshire. For there, in the heart of England, Sir Isaac Newton was born. From such simple origins his influence spread to change the world.

Childhood in Lincolnshire

Isaac Newton was born just after midnight on Christmas Day in 1642. He was premature and the doctor who attended his birth did not expect him to survive. His father, a fairly prosperous farmer, had died three months earlier, leaving Isaac's mother, Hannah, to raise the tiny boy on her own.

The Newton family were not poor – the Woolsthorpe manor house owned by Isaac's father was large and comfortable, but raising the sickly child alone could not have been easy for his mother.

At this time, England was in a state of tremendous upheaval. In 1629, the King, Charles I, had dissolved parliament because he wanted to rule the country in his own way, without having to abide by the law or take note of the people's wishes.

Charles I reigned in this way for eleven years, with opposition to him growing all the time. Throughout the country a feeling of anger was building up about such things as the introduction of new rules for the Church of England and the King unlawfully demanding money from the people.

In 1642, the year Isaac Newton was born, the Civil War started over just who should hold the power in the land – the King or Parliament.

There followed several bloody battles between the Parliamentarians and the Royalists, led by King Charles I. Isaac Newton was just six years old when the war ended. This division of the country would affect England throughout his life and he would become a forceful spokesman for the Protestants.

While the young Isaac was probably unaware of the events taking place around him, the sleepy countryside in which he lived saw two battles less than fifty miles from his home.

Most of Lincolnshire was in the hands of the Parliamentarians, but Isaac's family supported the King. They would have often found themselves

"Sir Isaac was always a sober, silent, thinking lad, and was never known scarce to play with the boys abroad, at their silly amusements; but would rather choose to be at home, even among the girls, and would frequently make little tables, cupboards, and other utensils for me and my playfellows, to set our babies and trinkets on."
Miss Storer, Isaac Newton's childhood girlfriend.

in danger as Parliamentarian troops marched straight past the Newton family home on their way north. The only way they could survive was to keep their Royalist views to themselves. Isaac can hardly have been affected by the political unrest – he was more affected by his mother's decision, when he was three years old, to remarry.

The hated stepfather

Her new husband was a wealthy clergyman, Barnabas Smith, who was Rector at the village of South Witham a few miles away from Woolsthorpe. This came at a very impressionable time in Isaac's childhood and, as he recalled to close friends many years later, he felt only jealousy and hatred for his new parent. But, far worse was to come. Isaac's new stepfather decreed that Hannah Newton was to leave her son to live with his grandmother at Woolsthorpe while she was to move to South Witham to look after her new husband and his young children.

Isaac never got on with his grandmother. Friends and colleagues very rarely heard him speak of her when he remembered his childhood. Some people have said that the trauma he experienced over his mother's marriage scarred him for life and accounted for his melancholy as a teenager and emotional upsets in later life.

He loathed Barnabas Smith for the rest of his life. When Isaac was older he began to keep a diary in which he poured out his feelings of hatred for the man. Even in old age, almost eighty years later, he would tell friends how he often dreamt of killing his stepfather and rescuing his mother from the "beast"

The England of Newton's childhood was a country in political turmoil. The English Civil War had begun shortly before his birth and raged until he was six. In January 1649, the War ended and the king, Charles I, was executed.

A fascination for machines

Isaac's childhood was a lonely time. He made very few friends and usually kept himself to himself. Quite often he would lock himself away in a back room at his grandmother's house where he would spend the day making models and kites, sundials and little mechanical devices.

Before long, Isaac became well-known in the district for his models. Local people and relatives were amazed by his skill at constructing exact replicas of carts and wheeled machines. On one occasion, when he was thirteen years old, he built a scale model of a windmill that had just been built in the village. It worked perfectly and he even managed to set the sails in motion by placing a mouse on a wheel inside. People joked that he could even mill corn inside the tiny device.

From these stories of Isaac's early ability with machines, it is easy to see how he worked so well on problems in physics when he was at Cambridge University. All through his life, Newton used his natural talent with his hands to build models and to make scientific instruments, not least when he made his first reflecting telescope and ground lens that he used in his famous experiments with light.

Schooldays

When Isaac was ten, his stepfather, Barnabas Smith, died and his mother Hannah returned to the house at Woolsthorpe. Two years later, Isaac went to Grantham grammar school nearby where he stayed with his uncle in the town.

Like many great scientists, Isaac made little impression at school. He was considered average by his teachers and unsociable by his classmates. Later he admitted that he ignored his work and spent most of his time making models and carrying out his own experiments.

Isaac was unpopular with the other boys at school. He was physically weak as a child and could not take part in the rough games and fights that were a part of daily life at school. A studious, silent boy he never made any friends. Instead of playing after lessons were over, he would rush home to his tiny room at the top of the house to make his models and furniture for the girls' dolls houses. Instead of being impressed by his skill the other boys were jealous of Isaac's ingenuity and scientific talent. This only made things worse. But just before

Isaac Newton aged twelve. This portrait gives an accurate impression of the boy. He was a melancholy youth who found it very difficult to make friends and spent most of his time alone when he was not at school. The artist has successfully captured the thoughtfulness and other-worldliness of the young Newton. It was at this time that he amused himself by making models and toys.

Above: Woolsthorpe
Manor, the house where
Isaac Newton was born.
Left: A scene from a
typical classroom in a
seventeenth century
school. It was at school
that Newton eventually
found the respect of the
other boys and his teachers
after beating the school
bully in a playground fight.

Even Isaac Newton wanted to tell the world that he had been here! At the time, his teachers would probably have been furious that the boy had carved his name on a window ledge at Grantham School. But, years later, when he had become a world-famous scientist, they preserved the inscription for the amusement of future generations.

"In the meantime Mr. Stokes, who had a great value for him, often strongly solicited his mother to return him to his learning, the proper channel of his inclinations. He told her it was a great loss to the world as well as a vain attempt to bury so promising a genius in rustic employment, which was notoriously opposite to his temper; that the only way whereby he could either preserve or raise his fortune must be by fitting him for the University."

W. Stukeley,
Newton's first biographer.

his fourteenth birthday, an important event occurred that changed everything.

Isaac got involved in a fight with the school bully. He was much bigger than Isaac and extremely unpopular among the other boys. Despite being small and quite frail, Isaac won the fight by great cunning and gave his rival a severe nose bleed. After his victory, Isaac was held in high esteem and it encouraged him to work even harder at school and to win it as an intellectual battle as well as a physical one. This worked so well that before long he became headboy, gaining the respect of the teachers as well as his schoolmates.

Farmer or scholar?

Despite this, in 1659, Hannah Newton decided to take her son away from Grantham grammar school to work on the family farm. If it were not for two remarkably fortunate facts, Isaac Newton may well have remained a farmer for the rest of his life. The first was that his great genius had already been recognized by two very important people, his uncle and the headmaster of Grantham – Henry Stokes. During his last few years at Grantham School, Isaac had become the star pupil and Henry Stokes considered him to be the best student that he had ever had. It was easy to see how intellectual Isaac had become; he was always reading scholarly books and .devising ingenious solutions to problems. He worked on the theories of early scientists finding answers to intriguing mathematical puzzles and scientific curiosities. But, despite his intellectual skills, Isaac was absent-minded and forgetful – often leaving the work on the farm unfinished. This led to the second reason … his mother became convinced that the young man was an absolutely hopeless farmer.

So after much persuasion and at the insistence of the two influential men in his life, in 1661, the eighteen-year-old Isaac was admitted to Cambridge University.

Isaac's mother, Hannah, was not poor, but she could not afford to support Isaac through university, so he joined as what was called a subsizar. This meant that he had to earn his keep by cleaning the rooms of paying scholars, serving at the high table, and doing menial jobs for his superiors. However, Newton forced himself to put up with these indignities. The important thing was that he had made it to university. It was the most important step in his life. Never again would he be forced to do a job that he hated – like farming. He would be surrounded by others of his own type, intellectuals and thinkers. And, in three short years he would graduate and be a true scientist.

Early days at Cambridge

He arrived in Cambridge on June 4. It was a perfect sunny day as he walked through the city and along the banks of the River Cam. He was in total awe of the grand college buildings which lie alongside the river with their majestic lawns stretching to the water's edge. Cambridge was not a large city and to anyone arriving from London it would seem a quaint, picturesque little town, but to Isaac it was a real shock. He had never been away from the Lincolnshire countryside, and Cambridge, with its six thousand inhabitants, was a dramatic change.

He set about preparing for his studies straight away. On his first day he purchased a lock for his desk, a bottle of ink, a notebook and a pound of candles which he would use to light his room as he worked through the evenings.

However, Isaac's enthusiasm was soon dampened as he realized that he had not really moved on from the rough, boyish life of school and that many of the other students were just like the boys he thought he had left in Woolsthorpe. As a strict protestant an important part of Isaac's religion was that he did not spend a lot of time drinking and gambling. At university, Newton was confronted with such things for the first time and he immediately gained a reputation for being a boring and very solemn young man.

However, he soon settled in and found a friend in a fellow protestant student, John Wickins, and

The Wren Library, Trinity College at about the time Newton was a student at Cambridge University. Although this looks a peaceful scene, Cambridge – with its loud students, merchants and other cityfolk – must have come as quite a culture shock to Newton. He had rarely ventured beyond the area surrounding the quiet Lincolnshire village of his birth.

the two of them shared rooms at Trinity College, Cambridge.

After a few months at university Isaac began to relax a little and to enjoy student life and the freedom it brought. He did not desert his faith, but gradually started to enjoy a visit to the tavern with John and a game of cards with his friends.

New ideas

It was at this time in his rooms in Cambridge that Newton began to formulate his early theories of forces and movement for which he would become famous. Here, too, he started to develop his ideas about the nature of light and how a specially-shaped piece of glass, called a prism, can split light into a rainbow from red to violet.

And it was in the cobbled streets of Cambridge and under the towering spires of the city that Isaac Newton first began to think about gravity and all the ideas for which he was to gain worldwide recognition in later years.

But first he had to find a way of thoroughly understanding these difficult ideas. To do this Newton knew that he would have to use very advanced mathematics. To solve the mysteries of the universe, he would have to learn everything he could about the subject. And, although he did not realize it then, he would have to invent his own mathematics – the calculus. For the moment, he had to continue with his college work and pass his exams in order to stay at Cambridge – and that was no mean feat. He would have to concentrate on the philosophy courses at the university and think through his ideas in his spare time. Only in that way could he gain the respect of his masters while later he would be able to show the world of science the way ahead for the next three hundred years.

A lucky find

One Sunday afternoon in the early spring of 1664, Isaac and John Wickins decided to visit a fair that had arrived in Cambridge. Among the side shows and novelty stalls, tricksters and performers,

Opposite: When Isaac Newton first arrived in Cambridge, he strongly disapproved of drinking and gambling, but gradually he relaxed his strict Protestant views. It would have been in taverns such as the one shown here that Isaac and his roommate, John Wickins, would have the occasional ale and enjoy a game of cards with other friends from the university.

"According to my own observation, tho' Sir Isaac was of a very serious and compos'd frame of mind, yet I have often seen him laugh, and that upon moderate occasions.... He usd a good many sayings, bordering on joke and wit. In company he behavd very agreably; courteous, affable, he was easily made to smile, if not to laugh.... He could be very agreable in company, and even sometime talkative."
W. Stukeley,
Newton's first biographer.

Newton began his researches into the properties of light after coming across a prism at a stall at a fair in Cambridge. In his first experiment, he discovered that when white light is shone through a prism it splits the light into a rainbow. He called this arrangement the spectrum. The light ranges from violet at the top to red at the bottom.

Newton made a find which was to have an enormous influence on both his future and the future of science. He was passing stalls and counters strewn with painted toys and trinkets, deep in conversation with John, when suddenly his eye was caught by a strange object glinting in the afternoon sun. It was a prism. He was struck by its beauty and fascinated by the smoothness of its surface. He immediately realized that he could carry out some useful experiments with it and bought it. Back in his rooms at Trinity he began to experiment with the prism that very afternoon.

The rainbow effect

First, he pulled the curtains across all the windows apart from one. Over the remaining window he placed a piece of cardboard. He had cut a tiny slit into the cardboard so that light could filter into the room from the bright sunshine outside. Then he stood back and watched the narrow beam of light entering the darkened room. Next, holding the prism up to the light, he let the beam enter one side of the prism and observed the different bands emerging from it and shining onto the white wall behind him. The natural light that had entered the prism was split like a rainbow; it could be seen there on the wall. It ranged from violet at the top through indigo, blue, green, yellow and orange with red right at the bottom.

Newton was fascinated. People had seen this phenomenon many times before, but no one had really investigated what caused it. Many believed that the rainbow effect was already contained inside the prism and was let out by shining sunlight on it. Scientists of the day realized that the glass was altering the light entering the prism, but they did not know why. A prism was little more than a novelty or an interesting toy, but to Newton it was a treasure trove and he wanted to know all its secrets.

More experiments

After he had produced the rainbow on his wall, what he called the spectrum, Newton set about experimenting on what he had observed. The first thing he did was to block off all the different bands coming out of the prism except one: red. All the others were cut out of the spectrum using a piece of cardboard with a narrow slit in it that only allowed the red beam through. Then he sat back and looked at the single red band on the wall wondering what to do next. What would happen, he thought, if he now passed this red beam through another prism? Would this then split into a rainbow just as the sunlight through his window had done?

He purchased another prism and placed it in the path of the red band of light, turning it to see what emerged from the other side. And there, coming from the far side of the prism, was nothing more than the red beam he had shone into it. There was no rainbow effect, just the single red beam. All that had happened was that it was a little bent from

"I keep the subject constantly before me, and wait 'till the first dawnings open slowly, by little and little, into a full and clear light."

Isaac Newton.

the path it had taken into the glass.

This could only mean one thing. Sunlight contained all the different shades of the spectrum – violet, indigo, blue, green, yellow, orange and red – and that was that. It was impossible to keep dividing light further and further. If red light was shone into the prism, only red light emerged. If blue light was allowed to enter the prism, only blue light came out the other side.

The first modern scientist

The amazing thing was that nobody had found this out before. Furthermore, it is difficult to say why. The simple fact is, that because prisms were considered to be toys, scientists never bothered to experiment with them. Those who had worked with them in the past had not taken things far enough to find out anything really useful and were content to marvel at the rainbow effect a prism produced. It required a genius of Newton's ability to take things a step further: to investigate why a rainbow emerged when white light was shone into the prism and then to see if the different shades could be separated endlessly, just as the first beam had been.

Newton recorded his findings and set about deciding what all this meant. He measured the width of each band, changed the distance of the prism from the wall and tested all the possibilities. Then and only then could he put all his findings into the mathematical language that allowed him to devise theories to explain what was going on.

This was typical of Isaac Newton. Not content with just making observations, he always translated what he saw into mathematical language and came up with general theories. This is what made him so different to other scientists of the time. Modern scientists use this method to do things and because he used it over three hundred years ago, Isaac Newton is seen as the first modern scientist.

Newton spent many months working with his prisms, devising more and more experiments in his rooms at Cambridge. At times he would over-work and on more than one occasion John Wickins found

Opposite: Newton became fascinated with the properties of the prism and conducted experiment after experiment in his rooms at Trinity College. By closing the curtains and casting the room into semi-darkness, the effects of the prism were much easier to observe. As an undergraduate he took the understanding of the way light behaves far beyond that of previous generations.

"I never knew him to take any recreation or pastime either in riding out to take the air, walking, bowling, or any other exercise whatever, thinking all hours lost that was not spent in his studies."
Dr. Humphrey Newton, Isaac Newton's assistant.

After producing the spectrum, Newton decided to pass light through a second prism. He observed white light re-emerging from the other side and rightly suggested that it had recombined the separate bands of light. This demonstrated that white light was made up of all the parts of the rainbow. To prove this, he constructed a circle made up of all the parts of a rainbow, like the one on the left, and spun it very quickly. As you can see on the right, this simulates the effect of the second prism and makes the circle appear white.

him sprawled out over the papers on his desk, having fallen asleep tussling with a particularly difficult problem. He often forgot his meals and his cat grew fat on eating the untouched food left to grow cold on the edge of his desk.

After concentrated efforts he reasoned that we see objects because light all around us is reflected, or bounces off, whatever we are looking at and this light arrives at sensors in our eyes. Then he went further. Based on his experiments, Isaac had discovered that visible light, the light that enables us to see the world, was made up of all the different shades of the rainbow. When these are mixed, we see white light. When one part of the spectrum is missing, the light no longer appears white – it is tinted.

Many scientists would have stopped there. But Isaac always worked on a problem until he felt there was nothing else to learn from it. Having established that light was made up of the different shades of the spectrum, he wanted to see if he could recombine them to make white light again.

He set up his piece of cardboard in the window and again allowed some light to pass through the slit. This light he passed into the prism just as he had done in his first experiment. Sure enough, there was the spectrum on the far wall again. This time though, instead of blocking off all but the red band, he let all the light from the first prism pass into his second prism placed close to the first. Then, with growing excitement, he looked around to the far side of the second prism to see what had happened. There it was – a single beam of white light emerging from the glass face of the second prism. He was probably the first person in history to bring together all the shades of the rainbow into a single beam of white light. He had unmade a rainbow!

"His breakfast consisted only of bread and butter and a tea made by boiling a bit of orange peel in water which he sweetened with sugar. He partook freely of wine only with dinner, and for the most part drank only water."

W. Stukeley,
Newton's first biographer.

The spinning circle

As if all this evidence was not enough, Newton performed one more experiment, just to make sure that his findings would be believed. He realized early on that the spectrum was not made up of equal amounts of each shade – in a rainbow, there is always more blue than red. So, he simulated, or copied, the way nature mixes a rainbow.

He made a small circle of cardboard about ten centimetres across and divided it into seven different-sized sectors. These sectors represented the seven visible bands of the rainbow, which he then painted into the different sectors. Next, he mounted the cardboard circle on a spindle and spun it round as quickly as he could.

Staring at it from a distance, it looked white! He had fooled his own eyes. Because the circle was spinning so quickly, the different shades in their correct proportions appeared to merge together and make white light.

Newton was ecstatic and allowed even more meals to go to waste as he spent long hours carefully writing up his findings in great detail to allow future generations to benefit from his discoveries.

A clearer view

Newton did not publish his work readily so most of his discoveries with light were not read until many years later, but even then other scientists were quick to take advantage of them.

In the seventeenth century, spectacles were a rarity worn only by the rich, but even so, they were of remarkably poor quality. Within a few decades of their publication, Newton's researches had helped to produce great improvements in the design of lens and the manufacture of spectacles.

The microscope had been invented over fifty years before Newton's birth, but it was a primitive device, producing only a fuzzy, blurred image. By the eighteenth century, application of Newton's discoveries had turned it into a far more sophisticated instrument which. This, in turn, led to breakthroughs in many areas of medicine and biology.

But, probably the most important result of Newton's work with light during those months in Cambridge was the creation of a whole new science – the science of spectroscopy – over a hundred years later. Spectroscopy is the study of the light emitted by the flames produced when a material is burned. The flames of a fire seem to have a myriad of different reds, purples and blues jumping among them. The reason for this is that when different materials are burned, they produce light made up of different amounts of each of the shades of the spectrum. By allowing this light to pass through a prism, scientists can split the light into its component parts, exactly as Newton had done with sunlight. In this way they can discover what chemicals are in the material that is being burned.

Flight from the Great Plague

Newton had made all these great discoveries before he had graduated. But then in April 1664, after three years' study, he became a scholar of the college. He was elevated from the position of subsizar and no longer had to perform the menial duties expected of him as a poor undergraduate.

A year later, in 1665, he was made a Bachelor of Arts, a title automatically awarded after four years at the university. This meant that he could spend four more years living at Trinity College, pursuing whatever areas of knowledge he wished to study.

Newton immediately embarked on developing his ideas about how light worked and at the same time began his researches into gravity and how the planets move in their courses.

However, his early experiments at Cambridge were to be interrupted. In the summer of 1665 a

The Great Plague of 1665 was one of the worst natural disasters in the history of England. The terrible disease struck down rich and poor, young and old, leaving in its wake a trail of horrible suffering and the stench of rotting bodies.

The Great Fire of London began on September 2, 1666, just before the Plague had completely died down. It started in a baker's shop in Pudding Lane in the heart of the City of London. From there, the fire spread to engulf the entire City and raged for four days before it burnt itself out. It left over thirteen thousand houses in ashes.

great calamity was about to descend on the country which nobody could prevent and against which there was precious little defence – the Great Plague was about to strike.

The plague began in London where people lived in cramped and extremely unhygienic conditions. It ravaged the city of London. Thousands of people were dying with horrible symptoms. Victims had a terrible fever and their bodies were covered with huge running sores before they slowly died in all-consuming pain. The corpses were collected and transported through the city in great wagons,

then buried in mass graves away from the main population. In some districts the dead and dying outnumbered the living. Then, during the hot months of 1665, the plague began to spread beyond the capital. People going outside London carried the dreadful disease to other cities and began to infect their populations. By June 1665, Cambridge had become too dangerous to live in and the university was closed down. Along with the other students, Newton left Cambridge. He moved back to Lincolnshire where he could continue with his studies at the manor house.

Back home

During the last year at Trinity, Newton had been working especially hard. After he had obtained his degree, he had more time to explore his own interests. The first hurdle to get over when developing his ideas was his lack of advanced mathematics.

Although the study of mathematics was an important part of his course there were very few mathematicians in the world who had developed anything like the techniques he needed. But there were some and he managed to track down their books in the great libraries at Cambridge.

Sorting through the shelves, Newton found works by the famous French philosopher and mathematician, René Descartes, and the British philosopher Henry More. These men were leaders of the "New Science", a bold and imaginative movement of thinkers spread across Europe who were trying to push back the frontiers of modern science and mathematics.

It would have amazed the twenty-three-year-old Isaac Newton if he were to be told that within a few short years, he would be one of the most respected members of this exclusive "club".

At Cambridge in early 1665, Newton read everything he could by these great thinkers and when he could not find what he needed for his early theories of light and mechanics, he could only do one thing – he created his own mathematics.

So it was that by the time the plague made Cambridge too dangerous a place to stay in, he had taken the first few steps towards cracking the problems of developing his theories. The peace and solitude of Lincolnshire served to nurture his inventive mood.

In late summer, the great breakthrough came, when the apple tree incident occurred, and Newton began to really get to grips with his theory of gravitation.

Gravity

At Cambridge he had been toying with the idea that some forces of nature act from a distance. The

René Descartes was probably the greatest French scientist and philosopher of the seventeenth century. Although he died when Newton was only seven, his work lived on after his death and represented the ideas of the "New Science" which laid the foundations for Newton's own monumental work. In particular, Descartes' discoveries in geometry proved to be a great influence on Newton while at Cambridge.

idea that one object could affect another without being connected by wires or strings was a strange one that very few scientists had imagined before. But the evidence was growing that there was a force which did this – the force that kept the planets in their paths, for instance. There was definitely some strange attraction between objects which was invisible to the eye but must exist. How else, Newton stated, could the planets stay orbiting around the sun, and the moon orbiting around the earth? There were no strings holding the earth and the moon together, so how could these things happen unless some unknown, unseen force was at work?

When the apple fell from the tree in his mother's garden and landed on the head of the young genius, Isaac knew that the apple had been pulled to the earth by the same invisible force that kept the planets and the moon in their orbits – the force of gravity. The earth was exerting a pulling force on the apple and dragged it to it, in the same way that the sun exerts a pulling force on the planets and the earth exerts a pulling force on the moon. But, if that was the case, why did the planets not crash into the sun and the moon smash into the earth in the same way that the apple had crashed to the ground?

The pail of water

Newton struggled with this problem for days, then, just as he was packing to return to university, the truth struck him. For some strange reason, at that very moment, he remembered a game played at school. All at once the memories came flooding back. They would each take turns to stand in the middle of the playground holding a rope that had been tied to the handle of a pail of water. The idea was to spin round the pail of water at the end of the rope as fast as you could. To win, you had to whirl the pail around your head without spilling a drop of water. Everyone was astonished how the water always stayed in the pail as it spun around.

That was just the inspired flash of memory he needed. Suddenly it all made sense. There was a

"What is important for Newton, he recognized his own capacity because he understood the significance of his achievements. He did not merely measure himself against the standard of Restoration Cambridge; he measured himself against the leaders of European science whose books he read."
    Richard Westfall, from his biography, "Never at Rest".

"After dinner, the weather being warm, we went into the garden and drank thea, under the shade of some apple trees, only he [Newton] and myself. Amidst other discourse, he told me, he was just in the same situation, as when formerly, the notion of gravitation came into his mind. It was occasion'd by the fall of an apple, as he sat in a contemplative mood. Why should that apple always descend perpendicularly to the ground, thought he to himself."
    W. Stukeley, Isaac Newton's first biographer.

NASA astronaut, Edward White, is floating, apparently weightless above the Earth. In orbit, objects (including humans) experience weightlessness because they are in "free fall" like a sky-diver.

reason why the planets remained in orbit instead of crashing toward the sun and why the water stayed in the pail instead of pouring out.

It was due to the sideways speed that the planets went at as they circled, or orbited, around. As for the pail of water, the tension of the rope pulling inwards forced the pail to travel in a circle but the water was obeying what

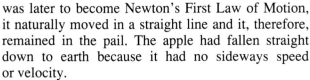

was later to become Newton's First Law of Motion, it naturally moved in a straight line and it, therefore, remained in the pail. The apple had fallen straight down to earth because it had no sideways speed or velocity.

Back to Cambridge

By 1667, the plague had subsided and Cambridge was deemed safe again. The university re-opened and in March Newton returned to his rooms in Trinity College.

When he had settled in, he began to work on the theory he had thought up just before leaving

Above left: An eighteenth century cartoon lampooning Newton's theory of gravity.

Above: The Space Shuttle Atlantis lifting off from the Kennedy Space Center. Despite the fact that the voyage of a spaceship relies on incredibly accurate calculations, Newton's theory of gravitation is used almost unchanged for programming them.

Lincolnshire. He wrote out mathematical formulae to see if his idea could work. After weeks of concentrated effort, he had completed the calculations and he was right. There was an invisible force at work that held the planets in their courses.

Not satisfied with this breakthrough, he wanted to know more about this mysterious force. He realized that the force of gravity must get weaker the further away each object was from the other. He knew, for instance, that planets furthest away from the sun must experience a weaker pull than those closer to the sun. But how did the strength change?

Using the advanced mathematics he had developed before leaving Cambridge, he worked out that if one planet was twice as far away from the sun as another, then it felt only a quarter of the force of gravity. If it was three times further away, it felt only one ninth of the force.

As the numbers appeared from his pen he instantly realized what this must mean. If his numbers were right, the force of gravity obeyed "an inverse square law". In other words, if the distance between objects was doubled, the force of attraction between them was a quarter of what it was before, as $2 \times 2 = 4$. If the distance was tripled, the force was one ninth, as $3 \times 3 = 9$. If the distance apart was four times greater, the force was one sixteenth the original size, because $4 \times 4 = 16$. The word inverse simply means that the 4, 9 or 16 go below the line in a fraction (in other words, they become the denominator of a fraction).

Fellowship

This discovery was a tremendous breakthrough. Scientists before him had imagined such an invisible force in nature, but nobody had managed to find out how it worked and less still how its strength changed at different distances.

Thanks to all this and his discoveries with light before the plague and his new mathematics, within six months of returning to Cambridge University, the twenty-five-year-old Newton was elected to the

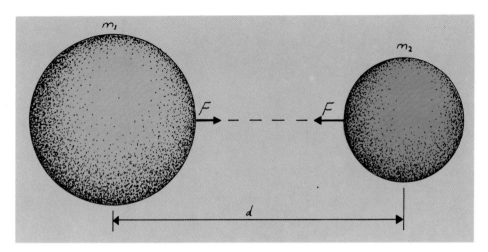

illustrious position of Fellow of Trinity College.

It was a meteoric rise and partly made possible by his growing friendship with the Professor of Mathematics at Trinity – Isaac Barrow. The two Isaacs made an odd pair. Barrow was extrovert and popular whereas Newton was shy and retiring. However, they worked together and became friends as well as colleagues. Barrow realized Newton's potential after seeing the work he had done during the plague years but it was the publication of a new work by a Danish mathematician, Nicolas Mercator, that brought Newton's genius to the attention of the rest of the scientific world.

In 1668, Mercator published a book of mathematics called *Logarithmotechnia*. A few weeks after it was published, Newton received a copy and began to read it. Within a couple of hours he was panic-stricken. Mercator was writing about the mathematics he, Isaac Newton, had discovered years earlier before the plague. Newton had recorded his findings, but had not published the results. The only person who knew that he had been first with the discovery was Professor Barrow.

What was he to do? He could not let another mathematician take the credit for all the work he had done before leaving Cambridge in 1665.

Most people would immediately have publicized the fact that they had made the discoveries three years before. But, in some ways Isaac Newton was

Above: Diagram illustrating Newton's law of gravity. The force of attraction between the bodies depends upon the mass of the bodies and the distance between them. This is represented by the equation $F = G\, m\, m\, /d^2$, where G is the power of gravity, m and m are the masses of the bodies and d is the distance between them.

a peculiar man. Like many geniuses, he did not approach things in the same way as most people. He was always cautious, even secretive, about letting other people see his work and this attitude remained with him in old age. But for the fact that his pride could not let him remain silent, he may never have got the credit for his mathematical discoveries.

Newton's plan

He had a plan. He asked Professor Barrow to publish his original manuscript anonymously and to circulate it among his powerful colleagues in London and Europe. Only when this paper was accepted as the original breakthrough would Barrow be allowed to announce the author's name.

So it was done. Within two days, Newton had the original manuscript tidied up and Professor Barrow saw that it was circulated. In this first published work, Newton explained his ideas in far greater detail than the mathematician Mercator had done in his book, and after a few weeks, the whole of the scientific community had accepted this version of the story. It was only then that the author's name was revealed and Isaac Newton became renowned for his mathematical breakthrough.

Professor of Mathematics

Not long after this, his friend and great supporter Isaac Barrow decided to retire as Professor of Mathematics at Trinity to pursue his private studies. He nominated Newton as his successor. The masters of the university agreed with his choice and, at the age of twenty-six, Isaac Newton became the youngest ever Professor of Mathematics at Cambridge.

The post was an important one. Now his work would be taken seriously and he would no longer need to resort to secret methods to convince people, as he had done with the Mercator episode.

But, Newton was not a genius at everything.

"Sir Isaac in mathematics could sometimes see almost by intuition, even without demonstration, as was the case in the famous proposition in his Principia, that all parallelograms circumscribed about the conjugate diameter of an ellips are equal....
William Whiston.

35

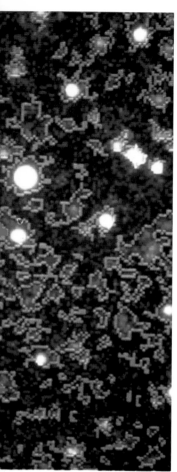

The job as professor required that he deliver lectures a few times a year, but he was a poor speaker. The attendances gradually fell and on one famous occasion he gave a lecture to an empty room, with only the walls as an audience!

Otherwise, the post suited him perfectly. It paid a reasonable salary and he only had to do a little teaching and attend occasional meetings and ceremonies. One of the greatest benefits of being Professor at Trinity was the freedom and time it gave him to carry out his own investigations.

Galileo's refracting telescope

The first telescope had been invented over sixty years earlier in 1608. Although he did not invent the device, the great Italian scientist, Galileo Galilei, made the instrument popular.

Galileo knew that light moved in straight lines. He also realized that when light from a distant object arrived at the surface of a lens it was bent by the glass of the lens. So, if an observer placed an eye on the other side of the lens, the light arriving at the eye appears to come from a much bigger object.

Galileo called his telescope a refracting telescope. It consisted of two lenses placed at either end of a tube. The lens at the far end of the tube is called the object lens and the one near the eye the eye lens. The object lens focuses light into the tube and the eye lens magnifies the distant object by bending the light coming from it.

This type of telescope worked very well and news of the invention spread far and wide. Within a few years, refracting telescopes were used by astronomers all over Europe to study the moon and the planets of the solar system.

A new type of telescope

In the early 1670s, Newton built a new type of telescope, a telescope altogether different from Galileo's and more powerful.

It consisted of a mirror placed at one end of

Opposite below: The telescope that Newton designed in the 1670s. Known as a reflecting telescope, it was far superior to the earlier refracting telescope made famous by Galileo. Above and opposite above: Galaxies millions of light years away from Earth. The development of sophisticated telescopes, based on Newton's principles, has enabled astronomers to see further into space than ever before.

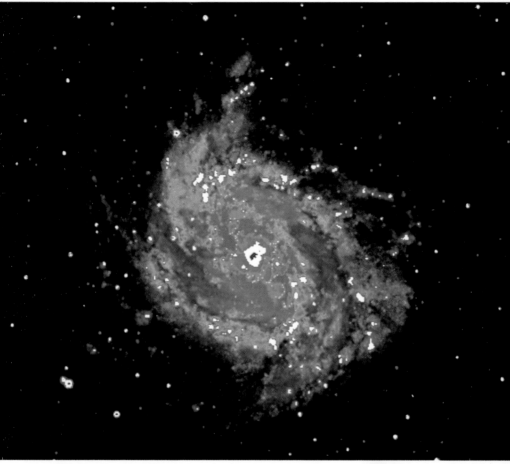

of a thick tube. The mirror was a special type called a concave mirror, which is curved. If you look at it from the front, it curves away from you – almost like looking into a tiny cave. Looking at it from the back, it appears to be bulging toward you.

Newton realized that if light from a distant object such as a planet, hit this special mirror it would bounce back to a point in front of it. The mirror produced the same effect as the eye lens in a refracting telescope. It made the light appear to come from a far nearer object. If the light was then reflected into an eyepiece at the side of the tube, the observer would see a magnified image of the planet. Newton called his telescope a reflecting telescope.

Newton's amazing new telescope was revolutionary and more powerful than most refracting telescopes – and he had made it with his own hands. He had ground the lens, shaped and polished the mirror, and built the tube. He had even designed and made his own tools! The skills he had learnt as a child building models and toys in Lincolnshire had come in very useful.

The Royal Society

Isaac Newton's reflecting telescope was a sensation, and if they were not already convinced, other great scientists of the day realized that they had a true genius in their midst. In early 1672, he was invited to join the distinguished Royal Society.

The Royal Society was a small circle of senior scientists who had formed themselves into a group in 1660, when Newton was only eighteen. They had the support of King Charles II, and among the membership were such important and famous men as the chemist, Robert Boyle, and the scientist and

The Royal Society began as an infrequent gathering of colleagues, but soon after Newton became President, it grew rapidly to become a highly respected and prestigious institution. Here we see a meeting of the Royal Society during the time of Newton's presidency. He is in the middle of the picture, chairing the proceedings.

architect who built London's St. Paul's Cathedral, Christopher Wren. An invitation to join their ranks was a great privilege and Newton jumped at the chance.

Disagreements

In February, soon after joining the Royal Society, thirty-year-old Isaac Newton delivered his first paper. This involved demonstrating one of his theories to an audience at the Society accompanied by a short publication. Newton chose to talk about his theory of light and the spectrum. It was at this first talk that he met and chatted to another great scientist of the day, Robert Hooke, who would later become the secretary of the Royal Society.

The two men were both highly-respected scientists and great personalities, but they approached science in totally different ways and never saw eye to eye. Each was convinced that their way was the right one.

Newton was always very careful and meticulous, chasing a problem until he had the answer and learning as much as he could from his researches. Hooke was an excellent scientist who worked on many different problems at once. However he did not explore each one in as much depth as Newton did.

This was not the only reason for their disagreements. There was the matter of professional rivalry.

Hooke considered himself to be the expert on light. He disagreed with Newton's theory and championed his own ideas. For the first time in his life, Isaac was confronted with a scientific equal. For many years the rows raged at the Royal Society and in the scientific community at large. And, from that very first meeting, the two men could never be friends and were often enemies.

Alchemy

Back in Cambridge, Newton carried on with his studies in private. The Royal Society took up little of his time and the muddy, pot-holed roads made travel in coaches, with wooden wheels, uncomfortable and tiring. He would only make the long journey to London when he had to, which was rare.

Because of all the arguments and squabbling, he decided to leave physics and mathematics for a while. Instead, he began to devote his time to furthering his researches into other areas of science. For many years the subject to occupy his thoughts most was alchemy – the forerunner of chemistry.

Alchemists were not scientists. They were more like magicians or witch doctors, intent on achieving the impossible – making potions to produce immortality, or love potions and magical cures. Newton would not have liked to be included among them. They were sloppy and messy with their work. They kept few records of their discoveries and did not really understand what they were doing. Newton was the opposite to this and the only reason he was getting involved with such things was that he had an endless thirst for knowledge. He wanted to know everything, and any area of study interested him.

The secrets of alchemy were elusive. He could see that the many amateurs who were working on the subject around the world were going about things in a terribly disorganized way. Newton was convinced that he could make a valuable contribution to this largely unexplored area of science.

The careful scientist

What made Newton so different from anyone else working in the area of alchemy was that he was incredibly meticulous and careful. He recorded all his discoveries and backed up all his ideas with experiments.

Many people think that Isaac Newton was the first "real scientist" because of his careful methods and because he used mathematics to describe the things he could prove from experiment. He was the first to do this, and many see him as the founder of modern science as we know it today.

Newton used his methods in his alchemy, but unlike his work in physics and mathematics, he made no great breakthroughs in chemistry. Day

after day, he would sit in his self-built laboratory at Trinity. He had constructed his own array of bottles and tubes, beakers and condensers, and devised experiment after experiment. But, he had little luck. The secrets of chemistry would always elude him, and after many years of research he achieved little.

Then, one warm June evening in 1679 something happened that altered the course of his life and brought an end to his alchemical studies. He was in the laboratory as usual, blending chemicals and mixing test tubes of solutions, when a knock came on the door. It was a messenger on horseback. He handed Newton an envelope containing a single sheet of paper. He opened it and read the contents. After quickly scanning the first few words, he knew the terrible truth. He must return to his home in Lincolnshire immediately; his mother, Hannah Newton, was dying.

Back in Lincolnshire

For the next six months Newton could not think of alchemy nor even his beloved physics and mathematics. His whole time was suddenly occupied by sorting out the affairs of his mother's estate. Apart from a young half-brother, Benjamin Smith, the son of his hated stepfather, he was the only other heir.

It took many months to sort out the maintenance of the manor and the farmland adjoined to it. Benjamin was an unreliable youth and could not be trusted with the running of the estate. To make things worse, the young man was ill and bedridden and Newton had to organize nursemaids as well as the general running of the farm. It was not until the beginning of 1680 that he was able to hand the estate over to a worthy manager and to return to scholarship and his experiments at Trinity.

"Newton ... was obsessed with the ideal of rigor and could hardly convince himself that anything was ready for publication."
Richard Westfall, from his biography, "Never at Rest".

A return to mechanics

Returning to Cambridge, Newton made a decision. He would put aside his alchemical experiments for a while. He had done as much as he could and needed to turn his hand to other things.

In London, arguments with Robert Hooke were becoming increasingly bitter. It was as much as Newton could do not to lose his temper in public. For most of the next few years, angry letters continued to pass between Hooke in London and Newton in Cambridge. And they grew more and more heated. Hooke could not accept the things Newton suggested and was forever stating that the things he did agree with, he had thought up first. This was to be the case with the laws of motion which Newton was working on.

Although they never rowed in public, letters between Newton and Hooke could be scathing. On one occasion, when Hooke had claimed that he had discovered Newton's theories first, Newton wrote to the Secretary of the Royal Society:

"Hooke has done nothing and yet written in such a way as if he knew and had sufficiently hinted all but what remained to be determined by the drudgery of calculations and observations, excusing

One of the things that distinguished Newton from most scientists before him was his meticulous way of working. He realized that science, and especially physics, was a very precise subject which had to be approached in a strictly disciplined way. Once an experiment was devised he would repeat it many times in order to eliminate errors or any possibility of chance – and then kept impeccable records of his findings.

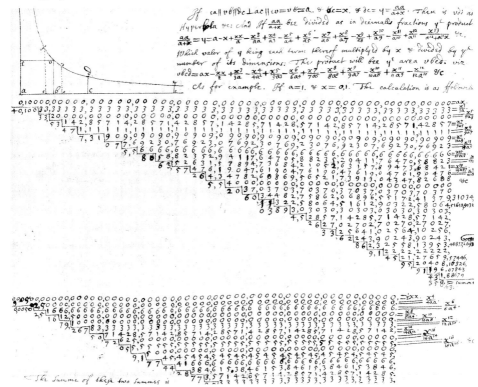

Newton's Laws of Motion in action. Here you can see the balls of a toy, called Newton's Cradle, colliding as they go through a periodic swing. The motion of the balls demonstrates the laws Newton encapsulated in the "Principia". The principles governing the motion of the balls are the same as those that dictate the way a racing car, a supersonic airliner or an interplanetary spacecraft behaves.

Opposite: The "Principia" has been described as the greatest work of science in history. In this single volume Newton laid down the foundations for the study of mechanics for the next three hundred years. His theories expressed within the "Principia" also captured the public's imagination. It was an immediate success within the scientific community throughout Europe and, within his own lifetime, Newton became widely accepted as Britain's greatest scientific genius.

himself from that labour by reason of his other business: whereas he should rather have excused himself by reason of his inability."

The two men very rarely met except at Royal Society meetings and even then there was usually a frosty silence between them. On one occasion Newton wrote to his friend Edmund Halley claiming that Hooke was no more than a "pretender", and a "grasper".

But, one good thing came from all this. Newton became so angry with Hooke's constant statements that he had been first to discover his theories of motion, that the proud man threw himself heart and soul into his researches.

Despite his pride and anger, Newton still found it difficult to allow his work to be published. His friends were constantly pushing him. "If you're so angry with Hooke," they said, "why not publish your work and bring him down in flames?" Newton always claimed that he was not ready. It seemed like nothing would change his mind. That was until his closest friend decided to intervene.

A persuasive friend

In May 1684, Newton's most trusted friend, the scientist Edmund Halley, made a special trip from his home in London to Cambridge. His mission was to persuade Newton once and for all to publish the results of his work on mechanics – the science of how objects moved, which he had been developing off and on since the Great Plague.

At first Newton was not convinced. He was not prepared to publish anything half-hearted or unfinished. But, Halley had a couple of tricks up his sleeve.

First, he suggested that Newton did not simply publish a small booklet of half-finished ideas. He had a far grander suggestion. He, Edmund Halley, would himself finance the publication of a book describing all the ideas he secretly knew his friend had formulated. Not only that, he also convinced Newton that, unless he moved quickly, others may beat him to it and there could be a repeat of the Mercator episode sixteen years earlier.

After much persuading, Edmund Halley left Cambridge with Newton's assurance that he would devote himself entirely to writing a full account of his greatest discoveries.

The pinnacle of scientific achievement

It took Newton two years to finish his book, working night and day to complete it. He hardly slept, and ate only when his hunger was so great that he could no longer concentrate.

On April 28, 1686, the book was finally ready. It was called *Philosophiae Naturalis Principia Mathematica*, but is usually referred to as the *Principia* (The Principles). It was delivered to the Royal Society that evening and excerpts were read to the gathered scientists, although the author himself decided not to attend.

To most of the scientists meeting at Arundel House, the home of the Royal Society, the book was a revelation. It described Newton's ideas of gravity, the centrifugal force and how the two are related. As well as these older ideas, there were plenty of new proposals. Most importantly, however, the *Principia* contained what became known as Newton's laws of motion.

Inertia

There are three laws of motion (see p.62) stated in the *Principia*, but the first, which deals with the concept of inertia, has the widest applications.

Inertia is the term given to the tendency for all objects to resist change or movement. In order to move an object, a force has to be applied to overcome its inertia. "Inertia" is used to describe a lazy person – lazy people have to overcome their inertia in order to do anything.

Newton stated that because of their inertia, all things continue in a state of rest or moving in a straight line unless affected by an outside force.

It is easy to see that this must be true. If a perfectly smooth ball was rolled along a perfectly smooth surface and there was no wind or any other force at work, the ball could, in theory, carry on rolling forever. Of course, in real life the ball would slow down and eventually stop, and that is caused by outside forces, such as friction and air currents.

Newton's immediate predecessor in the field of mechanics was the Italian physicist Galileo. He had studied the properties of falling objects, but no one before Newton had thought about why a force had to be applied to a stationary object in order to make it move.

New wisdom

Today, such notions as force and inertia are taken for granted. They seem obvious. In Newton's time, the notion of forces and the application of energy to overcome the inertia of stationary objects was a totally new idea.

A thousand years before Newton's time, the Greek philosopher, Leucippus, had proposed the theory of causality. "Nothing happens without a cause, but everything with a cause and by necessity."

It seems an obvious statement but it is terribly vague. What Newton did was to explain the idea that forces need to act on an object and to cause the effect of overcoming inertia or changing the object's path. He proved this idea using geometry and predicted the effect caused by the application of forces of various strengths on different objects. This is where Newton's "real" science was so different to the philosophies of the Greeks and the pseudo-scientists up to Galileo's time.

Newton laid down laws that could be applied to predict events with remarkable accuracy. Newton's mechanics was systematic, it was built on sound fundamental principles and simple, irrefutable laws which could be applied to the most elaborate and complex problems – problems such as sending spaceships to the planets, or something as relatively simple as the movements of a billiard ball on a smooth surface.

What was really revolutionary about Newton's discoveries was the idea that an object moves or

"So intent, so serious upon his studies that he ate very sparingly, nay, ofttimes he has forgot to eat at all, so that, going into his chamber, I have found his mess untouched, of which, when I have reminded him, he would reply – 'Have I!' and then making to the table, would eat a bit or two standing, for I cannot say I ever saw him sit at table by himself...."
Dr. Humphrey Newton,
Isaac Newton's assistant.

changes course because of *external* forces acting upon it and not due to a consequence of an *internal* change within the object itself. A jet aircraft moves by obeying Newton's Third Law, "For every action, there is an equal and opposite reaction." A force thrusts combustion gases backwards out of the engines while an equal and opposite force pushes the aircraft forwards.

A practical concept

Within a few years of the publication of the *Principia,* the idea of inertia, along with the consequences of the other two laws, had started to transform the world for other scientists and engineers. They incorporated Newton's laws in designs for machines and scientific equipment, clocks and wheeled devices, anything that involved moving parts. The laws made it possible to work out whether a machine would function properly before it was even built.

From that time, scientific thinking changed fundamentally – it would *never* be the same again.

Opposite and above: Modern day applications of Newton's theories extend into all areas of science and engineering. These pictures show everyday examples of modern engineering which rely on the laws of mechanics and dynamics expressed by Newton in the "Principia". The vast technical knowledge needed to design and build suspension bridges and towering skyscrapers is based on the principles Newton set out over three centuries ago. And, without an understanding of the laws of motion, the steam engine would never have stayed on the rails.

Isaac Newton had laid the foundations for a whole new era of scientific invention, paving the way for the great industrial revolution. It was Newton's laws of motion that made it possible for the British engineer, Isambard Kingdom Brunel, to build his enormous steamships and suspension bridges in the nineteenth century. Without Newton's laws of motion, James Watt could not have constructed the first working steam engine less than one hundred years after the publication of the *Principia* and the rail networks would never have been built.

Modern applications

Architects and builders also gained from the *Principia*. Newton's laws of forces help to solve the problems of building modern structures and massive skyscrapers like the Empire State Building in New York.

Newton's laws are still the basis of modern mechanical engineering. They are used by people working in almost every field of science, from oil well technicians to space engineers, car designers to satellite constructors.

When rockets travel to the moon they use the principle of inertia exactly as it was described in the *Principia*. The rocket is launched into earth's orbit using powerful engines, but in space there is no friction or air to slow it down. So, engineers at mission control simply fire a tiny booster engine on the side of the ship, called a retro rocket, and this sets the spaceship on course to the moon. Because all objects continue moving in a straight line until affected by an outside force, the rocket just keeps on going until it reaches the moon. After that initial burn no more thrust is needed and of course no more fuel. In fact, it is so easy to move in space that the rocket would crash into the moon if it was not slowed down by firing another booster as it approaches the surface.

Isaac Newton's *Principia* achieved nothing less than describing the laws of motion that work throughout the universe – the very laws which describe how the planets move, and the stars and galaxies stay in their courses. So great is the *Principia* that it has been said to be the pinnacle of scientific achievement, the greatest work of science in history.

There was one man, however, who did not see it that way – Robert Hooke.

From that very night, April 28, 1686, Robert Hooke attacked Newton over the contents of the *Principia*. He claimed that Newton had stolen his ideas of gravity and that he, Robert Hooke, had devised the inverse square law of gravity which was the central pillar of Newton's work.

Each rival had his followers at the Royal Society and in the rest of the scientific community in Europe. But after months of wrangling and fierce arguments in letters, Isaac won the day and Robert Hooke's suggestions were discredited by most scientists.

"'The Scientific Revolution' was so important to the development of mankind that modern historians honour the phrase with initial capital letters. The new way of seeing the world that it introduced first tentatively surfaced with the publication of Copernicus's work in 1543. It reached its triumphal acceptance with the appearance in 1687 of Isaac Newton's Principia."

From "The History of Scientific Discovery", edited by Jack Meadows.

The black years

For many years after the publication of the *Principia*, there was a silence from the Trinity rooms in Cambridge. Newton busied himself with his renewed interest in alchemy and there were no new works of such profound importance. All over Europe, the *Principia* was, and still is, acclaimed as the greatest work of science ever written. Its author became world famous not only among scientists but to the general population – thanks to the interest his book caused among poets, journalists and teachers.

Most people could not understand the mathematics in the book, but through simplified versions and word of mouth, the basic ideas contained in the *Principia* spread far and wide.

But the author, the great scientist himself, was not well. For many years he had been overworking, pushing himself to the limits of endurance, and now, at the age of fifty-one, it was taking its toll.

Nobody really knows what illness Newton suffered from between 1693 and 1696. Some claimed that he had had a nervous breakdown, others that he was simply exhausted physically. Whatever the

The stamping room in the Mint at the Tower of London. During Newton's time at the Mint, he made sweeping changes to the methods used to purify the metals used in the manufacture of coins. He was also in charge of prosecuting the infamous "clippers" who stole tiny pieces at the edges of coins. It is said that Newton took perverse pleasure in bringing these criminals to trial and, in many cases, execution.

cause, those years were later seen by the man himself as the worst period in his life. A time he referred to as "the black years". It was a time when he achieved little in physics, made no real progress in alchemy and suffered one bout of illness after another.

His friends rallied around him. Halley wrote frequently, as did others at the Royal Society and colleagues in London. All this support gradually helped him out of his black mood and physical sickness. But, the real turning point came in 1696 when he was made an offer that would change his life completely. He was invited to take up the important position of Warden of the Royal Mint.

Newton had lived in Cambridge University for thirty-five years when the call came from the Treasury to join the Royal Mint.

He accepted the offer immediately and so began the next phase of the great man's life. For a while he left scientific research altogether and launched himself into a new career as a high-ranking administrator in the capital.

The post at the Royal Mint was meant to be a reward for his scientific achievements and was really only seen as a prestigious honorary title, but Newton could never do anything by halves. He threw himself into his new job with enormous energy, far exceeding the expectations of his superiors at the Treasury.

As it happened, the job came at an important time. England was changing its coinage which had been badly affected by the Civil War years. It was severely in need of updating and improving, and Newton turned out to be just the man to make

Above is a Queen Anne coin, one of those struck under Newton's Mastership.

the change-over run smoothly. He supervised the pressing of the new coins and made sure that the money was distributed to the various banks around the country.

Clippers and thieves

Another aspect of Newton's job was the hunting down and prosecution of counterfeiters and a group of thieves known as "clippers". These were people who clipped off small pieces of coins, melted down the metal and extracted the silver.

Newton applied all his cunning, used so effectively to solve scientific problems, in tracking down these criminals and bringing them to justice. He was so successful that within three years of his appointment, in 1699, he was made Master of the Mint.

The scientific Warden

Of all Isaac's responsibilities at the Royal Mint, the most important was the essential task of testing the purity of the coins. All the coins had to be of the same weight and each had to contain exactly the same quantity of precious metal. The job of making sure that each coin turned out the same was not an easy one, but Newton's strict scientific training proved useful once again.

Each day he visited the pressing plant next to his offices at the Royal Mint. Using specially-designed ladles, workmen would take out a small sample of the molten metal. It would then be taken back to the warden's laboratory where he conducted chemical experiments on the metal to make sure that it was of the required purity.

High office

For years Newton had paid little attention to research. He had kept his professorship at Cambridge until he was made Master of the Royal Mint, but he no longer lectured and conducted very few experiments because the demands of his new career were so great.

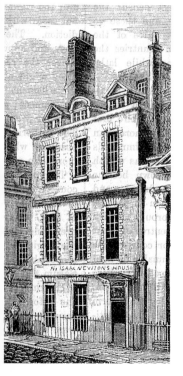

In becoming Master of the Royal Mint, Newton had established himself as a senior civil servant. He lived in this rather grand house near Leicester Square in London. In middle age, he was seen as a pillar of the establishment and a highly-regarded politician. Knighted in 1705, Newton was said to have substantial influence at the Royal Court and commanded the Royal Family's greatest respect.

Sir Isaac Newton's House

The Royal Society was going through a confused time in its history and there were many arguments among its leading members as to the direction it should take. Newton only attended meetings once in a while partly because of his other interests and partly because of the continuing arguments between himself and Robert Hooke. But, in 1703, his rival and antagonist, the sixty-eight year old Robert Hook, died.

Without further ado, the members of the Royal Society voted to make their most famous and respected member its new leader. So, in 1703 at the age of sixty, Isaac Newton became the President of the Royal Society.

Newton worked hard to resolve the problems of the Society and undertook his responsibilities with the same determination and energy with which he approached everything. For a number of years, the Royal Society had been presided over by leading politicians who were not interested in the Society's aims. The weekly meetings were no longer concerned with matters of scientific interest that had been the reason for the Society being formed in 1660. When Newton took over as President, the membership was at an all time low. Having devoted his life to the Society's goals, Newton was determined to revive interest in the Society. He devised a "Scheme for establishing the Royal Society" to get it back on course again. In the "Scheme", he said that the weekly meetings must provide serious discussion for the members and only those with established scientific reputations would be allowed to give demonstrations at the meetings.

During Newton's time as President, attendances at the meetings more than doubled and from that time the Royal Society went from strength to strength. Newton managed to transform it from a small group of scientific colleagues to the world-famous and respected Society it is today.

A new publication

Newton was riding high. He was an internationally-renowned scientist, Master of the Royal Mint and President of the Royal Society. The *Principia* was

"Even when he was an old man the servants had to call him to dinner half an hour before it was ready, and when he came down, if he chanced to see a book or a paper, he would let his dinner stand for hours. He ate the gruel or milk with eggs prepared for his supper cold for breakfast."
John Conduitt,
a close friend of Isaac Newton.

The London of Newton's time. This picture was painted about 1690 shortly before he moved from Cambridge. By then the areas of the city destroyed by the Great Fire of London had been rebuilt. Many of the new buildings were constructed in stone rather than duplicating those built of wood which had been swept away by the flames. In the distance can be seen the Tower of London where Newton took up his position at the Mint in 1696.

finding more and more enthusiastic readers every year, its strength growing in the eyes of scientists all over the world.

In 1704, only a few months after becoming President of the Royal Society, Newton was persuaded to publish the work he had begun when he was an undergraduate at Cambridge – his discoveries with light. This branch of physics is called optics, and when he was ready to publish his studies in the spring of that year, he simply called his book *Opticks*.

It was another runaway success, and this time his enemy Robert Hooke was not around to ruin the acclaim. Once more, Isaac Newton was triumphant and the world was reminded, yet again, of the great man's genius. The President of the Royal Society was being hailed worldwide as the greatest scientist who had ever lived.

The final years

And so Isaac Newton continued to rule supreme in the world of science.

For twenty-three more years he retained his illustrious posts in both science and the Civil Service. He published no more great works, but then, he had already given the world two of the greatest works of science in two totally different areas of physics.

The year after *Opticks* was published, Isaac Newton was knighted by Queen Anne for his great works in both science and public service. He was the first scientist to be rewarded in this way.

Meanwhile he had made new enemies. There were others who were not put off by the way Robert Hooke had been defeated by Newton's acclaim. In his last years, as an old man in his late seventies,

"Fortunate Newton, happy childhood of science! He who has time and tranquility, can by reading this book live again the wonderful events which the great Newton experienced in his young days. Nature to him was an open book, whose letters he could read without effort."

Albert Einstein,
from the foreword to the
1931 edition of "Optics".

he was involved in public arguments with two other famous scientists of the day. The worst of these rows was that between Newton and the German scientist, Gottfried Leibniz. Leibniz claimed that he, and not Newton, had invented the branch of mathematics known as calculus. Newton had used this new form of mathematics nearly sixty years earlier when he was first developing his notions of mechanics and optics, but the argument had only just come to light, prompted by its use in the world famous *Opticks*.

Poor Leibniz did not really have a chance against a man so fierce as Newton. Isaac's forceful and argumentative character had hardened further still as he had grown older. Not only that, but he was also the greatest scientist in the world, leader of the most successful and respected scientific society on earth and a knight.

Newton again won the day by persuading his colleagues that Leibniz had first seen the calculus in his early publications and had copied the idea from him. In this way he obtained the agreement of the scientific world that he and not Leibniz was the first to formulate the calculus. Although Leibniz is remembered for his contribution to the invention and for many other branches of physics in which he worked, he died without riches or the power and awards bestowed upon his British rival.

Newton's legacy

Sir Isaac Newton died on March 20, 1727 aged eighty-four, having been ill and bedridden for several months. He was buried among the kings and queens, dukes and earls of England in London's Westminster Abbey on April 4.

So respected had he become during his life that for a week before the funeral, he had lain in state in the Abbey, a mark of respect usually reserved for monarchs. At the funeral, Newton's coffin was carried by two dukes, three earls and the Lord Chancellor.

It is difficult to exaggerate Sir Isaac Newton's contribution to science. To many, he was the

"He has become for me ... one of the tiny handful of supreme geniuses who have shaped the categories of the human intellect."
Richard Westfall, from his biography, "Never at Rest".

"I don't know what I may seem to the world, but, as to myself, I seem to have been only like a boy playing on the sea shore, and diverting myself in now and then finding a smoother pebble or a prettier shell than ordinary, whilst the great ocean of truth lay all undiscovered before me."
Isaac Newton.

Many paintings and sculptures of Newton were made during the great man's lifetime and after his death in 1727. Artists from all over Europe undertook commissions to commemorate the passing of England's most famous scientist. This marble sculpture, by Louis Francis Roubilliac, can be found today in the antechapel of Trinity College, Cambridge.

greatest scientist who ever lived. He was certainly a difficult and argumentative man who could never tolerate disagreement. He fought tooth and nail with his rivals and always won. There were many who disliked him.

He was seen as growing increasingly eccentric in his old age. He became obsessed with having his portrait painted and insisted on a new one every two or three years–which accounts for the unusually large number of well-painted portraits of the elderly Newton which have survived to the present day.

Many never forgave him for his treatment of his fellow scientists, and claimed that Newton did not give others due credit for their work. They implied that Newton had enjoyed sending criminals to their deaths while at the Royal Mint and suggested that he had manipulated influential people in order to succeed. All of these may be founded in truth, but we should also remember that he was a generous

These five stamps, from all over the world, celebrate the works of Isaac Newton and how they have changed our society. Newton's discoveries are remembered internationally by attaching his name to innumerable things from streets and buildings to telescopes and academic buildings.

man and often helped poor families, gave large sums to charity and never failed to provide financial help to distant relatives in troubled times.

He never married and had no heirs and his estate was taken over by the descendants of his stepfather, Barnabas Smith. But, Newton left far more to the world than simple property. He created a new approach to science and a totally original way of answering the questions we all wonder at.

Today, over three-hundred-and-fifty years after his birth, scientists around the world and in all areas of study still use the principles and ideas laid down by this amazing man. What greater legacy could any person ever leave?

Important Dates

1642   Aug: The English Civil War breaks out and continues until 1649.
Dec 25: Isaac Newton is born in Woolsthorpe, England, to Hannah Newton. His father had died three months earlier.

1655   Isaac Newton, aged twelve, starts at Grantham grammar school.

1661   June: Isaac Newton, aged eighteen, enters Cambridge University.

1664   Spring: Isaac Newton, aged twenty-one, begins his experiments with light.

1665   Isaac Newton becomes a Bachelor of Arts and begins to develop his own advanced mathematics.
The Great Plague breaks out in London and spreads to other cities.
Newton leaves Cambridge and returns to Woolsthorpe.

1666   Isaac Newton makes great breakthroughs in understanding the laws of gravity.
Sept 2-6: The Great Fire of London.

1667   Mar: Isaac Newton returns to Cambridge University. Within six months, he is elected Fellow of Trinity College.

1669   July: Isaac Newton's work, *De Analysis*, is circulated.
Oct: Isaac Newton is appointed Lucasian Professor of Mathematics at Cambridge University. Aged twenty-six, he is the youngest ever to hold the post.

1670-1   Isaac Newton develops his reflecting telescope.

1672   Isaac Newton is invited to join the Royal Society, a group of senior scientists.
Feb: Newton delivers his first paper to the Society.

1679   June: Isaac Newton's mother, Hannah, dies.

1684   Isaac Newton begins work on his book, *Philosophiae Naturalis Principia Mathematica*, usually referred to as the *Principia*.

1686   April 28: Extracts from the *Principia* are read at the Royal Society. The book is seen as a revelation in scientific circles.

1689   Isaac Newton is elected to represent Cambridge University in the "Convention Parliament".

1693-96   Isaac Newton suffers from a mystery illness.

1696   Mar: Recovered from his illness, Isaac Newton accepts the position of Warden of the Royal Mint.

1699   Dec: Aged forty-seven, Isaac Newton is made Master of the Royal Mint.

1701   Isaac Newton is elected Member of Parliament for Cambridge University.

1703   Nov 30: Isaac Newton is elected President of the Royal Society.

1704   Newton's book on his discoveries with light, *Optics*, is published.

1705   Isaac Newton is knighted by Queen Anne. He is the first scientist to receive the award.

1727   Mar 20: Sir Isaac Newton, aged eighty-four, dies.

Newton's Laws of Motion

1. Every body continues in a state of rest or uniform motion in a straight line unless it is acted on by an external force.

2. When a force acts on a body, the rate of change of momentum of the body is proportional to the force and changes in the direction in which the force acts.

3. To every action there is an equal and opposite reaction.

Newton's Law of Gravitation

All bodies in the universe attract each other with a force that is directly proportional to the product of the masses of the bodies and inversely proportional to the square of the distance between them.

Further Reading

Bronowski, J.: *The Ascent of Man*, BBC Books, London.
An adult book that deals with the history of science and technology. It has one chapter devoted to Newton and shows how his work influenced the progress of western civilization.

Fauvel, et al (ed.): *Let Newton Be*, Oxford University Press.
A richly-illustrated book, packed with information about Newton's life and work. More suitable for advanced students as the complex language makes it difficult to read in places.

Meadows, Jack (ed.): *The History of Scientific Discovery*, Harrap, London.
A beautiful book dealing with the lives and work of twelve great scientists, including Isaac Newton.

Moore, L.T.: *Isaac Newton, a Biography*, Dover.
One of the standard biographies. Use the index to browse.

Whyman, Kathryn: *Rainbows to Lasers*, ("Hands on Science" series), Franklin Watts, London.
An excellent book, full of information about how light behaves. It is illustrated throughout and gives simple experiments for younger readers to try.

Scientific Terms

Astronomy: The scientific study of the heavenly bodies, particularly their movements, positions, composition and distribution.

Binomial: In mathematics, an expression consisting of two terms that are connected by a plus or minus sign – e.g. $a+b$, $x-y$.

Binomial theorem: A *formula*, discovered by Isaac Newton, for finding any power of a *binomial* expression without using lengthy multiplication.

Biology: The science of life and living organisms, covering the study of their structure, function, growth, origin, ecology, evolution and distribution.

Calculus: The branch of mathematics that allows continuously varying quantities to be manipulated. It is used by engineers and scientists to solve problems involving such things as changing speeds and fluctuating currents in electrical circuits. Calculus originated with Archimedes, but was greatly advanced by Isaac Newton.

Centrifugal force: The apparent tendency of a spinning body to move outward from the middle of its axis of rotation.

Combustion: A chemical reaction in which a substance is mixed, usually, with oxygen and produces heat, light and flame. In a car engine – an internal combustion engine – petroleum is mixed with air and ignited to generate power.

Condenser: In chemistry, an apparatus for changing a substance in its gaseous state into a liquid.

Force: An influence that is capable of changing a body's state of rest or uniform motion in a straight line. A force can act from the outside or the inside.

Formula: In mathematics and physics, a statement or law expressed using symbols. In chemistry, symbols that represent the composition of a substance – e.g. H_2O is the chemical formula for water.

Friction: A *force* that resists the movement of one surface against another with which it is in contact.

Geometry: The branch of mathematics concerned with the properties, measurement and relationship of lines, points, angles, surfaces and solids.

Gravity: The *force* of attraction exerted by the Earth, or another planet or satellite, on bodies on or near its surface.

Laser: (**L**ight **A**mplification by **S**timulated **E**mission of **R**adiation) A device that produces a narrow, powerful, highly directional beam of light. The light is very bright and can travel over long distances without being dispersed.

Mass: The amount of material in an object.

Mechanics: The branch of physics concerned with the study of moving objects and the *forces* acting upon them.

Optics: The scientific study of light and vision.

Prism: In *optics*, a triangular block of glass or plastic used to disperse light or to change its direction.

Spectrum: The rainbow-effect produced when a beam of light is passed through a *prism*.

Spectroscopy: The study of the *spectrum*.

Theorem: In mathematics, a rule usually expressed as a *formula* – e.g. *binomial theorem*. Also, a proposition that has been, or can be, proved by reasoning.

Velocity: The speed at which an object travels in a particular direction.

Index

Alchemy 40-1

Barrow, Professor Isaac 33
Binomial theorem 6, **63**

Calculus 6, 17, 59, **63**
Centrifugal force 30, **63**
Civil War (English) 10-11, 53

Galileo 36, 47
Gravitation, law of 62
Gravity, theory of 5, 9, 17,
28-32
inverse square law and 32
Great Fire of London 5
Great Plague 5, 25-7, 45

Hooke, Robert 39, 43, 51,
55, 56

Inverse square law 32

Laws of motion see Motion,
laws of
Leibniz, Gottfried 58
Light
Newton's experiments
with 17-23
Logarithmotechnica 33

Mercator, Nicolas 33
"Miraculous Year, The" 5-6,
7, 27-8
Motion, laws of 8-9, 46-8, 62
effects of on science 49-51

"New Science" 28
Newton, Hannah 10, 11, 14,
42
Newton, Sir Isaac
and alchemy 39-42
argument with Leibniz 58
becomes Bachelor of Arts
58
becomes Professor of
Mathematics 35-6
becomes student 14-17
birth 10
childhood 10-14
death 58
death of mother 42
develops new
mathematics 6, 17, 28,
32, 33-5
develops reflecting
telescope 36-8

disagreements with
Hooke 39, 42-4, 51, 55
elected Fellow of Trinity
College 32-3
experiments with light
17-23
ill health 51-2
influence of his work on
science 6, 7-10, 24, 47,
49-50
joins Royal Society 38-9
becomes president of
55
and "Miraculous Year"
5-6, 7, 28-9
and Laws of Motion 8,
46-9
and Nicolas Mercator
33-5, 45
publishes *Opticks* 57
receives knighthood 57
relationship with
stepfather 11
at Royal Mint 52-4
and theory of gravity 5, 9,
17, 28-32, 46
writes and publishes *The
Principia*

Opticks 57, 58

Principia, The 46, 49, 50, 51

Royal Mint, The 53, 54, 55,
59
Newton appointed
Warden of 52
Newton becomes Master
of 55
Royal Society, The 43, 44,
46, 52, 55
Newton becomes
member of 38-9
Newton becomes
president of 55

Spectroscopy 24, **63**

Telescope, the
Galileo's refracting 36
Newton's reflecting 36-7
Theory of gravity see
Gravity, theory of